Facts About Countries
Great Britain

Clare Oliver

FRANKLIN WATTS
LONDON • SYDNEY

First published in 2005 by
Franklin Watts
96 Leonard Street, London
EC2A 4XD

Franklin Watts Australia
Level 17/207 Kent Street
Sydney NSW 2000

Facts About Countries is based on the Country
Files series published by Franklin Watts. It is
produced for Franklin Watts by Bender
Richardson White, PO Box 266, Uxbridge, UK.
Editor: Lionel Bender
Designer and Page Make-up: Ben White
Picture Researcher: Cathy Stastny
Cover Make-up: Mike Pilley, Radius
Production: Kim Richardson

Graphics and Maps: Stefan Chabluk
Educational Advisor: Prue Goodwin, Institute of
Education, The University of Reading
Consultant: Dr Terry Jennings, a former
geography teacher and university lecturer. He is
now a full-time writer of children's geography
and science books.

A CIP catalogue record for this book is available
from the British Library.

ISBN 0-7496-6034-1
Dewey Classification 919.1

Printed in China

Picture Credits

Pages: 1: PhotoDisc Inc./Jeremy Hoare. 3: PhotoDisc
Inc./Andrew Ward/Life File. 4: PhotoDisc Inc/Colin
Paterson. 6: Hutchison Photo Library/Robert Francis.
8: Hutchison Photo Library/Jeremy Horner.
9: Hutchison Photo Library/Peter Morzynski. 10 top:
PhotoDisc Inc./Andrew Ward/Life File. 10-11 bottom:
PhotoDisc Inc./Jeremy Hoare. 12 DAS Photo/David
Simson. 14-15 bottom: Hutchison Photo Library.
16-17: Eye Ubiquitous/G. Daniels. 18 top: John
Walmsley Photography. 18 bottom: Ted Spiegal/Corbis
Images. 20: Hutchison Photo Library/Bernard Gérard.
21: Eye Ubiquitous/Martin Foyle. 22: Hutchison Photo
Library/Bernard Gérard. 23: PhotoDisc Inc./Andrew
Ward/Life File. 24: Peter Tumley/Corbis Images. 26
PhotoDisc Inc./Andrew Ward/Life File. 28: Reuters
NewMedia Inc./Corbis Images. 29: Howard
Davis/Corbis Images. 30: PhotoDisc Inc./John Wang.
31: PhotoDisc Inc./Andrew Ward/Life File.
Cover photo: Digital Vision.

The Author

Clare Oliver is a full-time writer and editor of non-fiction books. She has written more than 50 books for children. This is her second book about Great Britain.

Note to parents and teachers

Every effort has been made by the Publishers to ensure that the websites in this book are suitable for children, that they are of the highest educational value, and that they contain no inappropriate or offensive material. However, because of the nature of the Internet, it is impossible to guarantee that the contents of these sites will not be altered. We strongly advise that Internet access is supervised by a responsible adult.

Contents

Welcome to Great Britain

Great Britain is made up of the kingdoms of England and Scotland and the principality of Wales. Together with the province of Northern Ireland, it is part of the United Kingdom (UK).

Worldwide influence

Great Britain was the first nation in the world to make its wealth from industry and manufacturing rather than farming. Despite being small, until the early 20th century Great Britain had a large empire. Today it is a member of the European Union (EU) and United Nations (UN) and still plays a important part in world events.

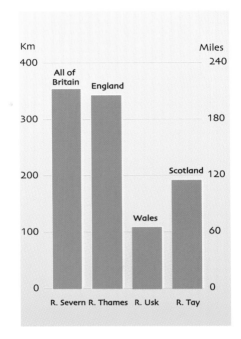

Above. **The length of Britain's longest rivers. The River Severn runs through England and Wales.**

Below. **Many castles in Great Britain – like this one in Scotland – date back more than 400 years, before England, Scotland and Wales joined.**

The Land

Britain's landscape varies from gentle hills to steep mountains. A mild, wet climate keeps much of the land fertile.

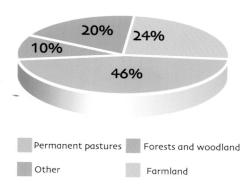

20%   24%
10%
46%

Permanent pastures · Forests and woodland
Other · Farmland

Above. **How land is used in Great Britain.**

Below. **Typical countryside in southern England.**

Rainfall

The wettest places are the highlands of Scotland, the Lake District and Snowdonia. All of these get more than 30 centimetres of rain each year. The east of Britain is much drier. Some places there get less than 7 centimetres of rain in a year.

Landscape and temperature

The middle part of Scotland consists of low hills and is mostly farmland. Towards Scotland's border with England, the land rises. Northern England is rugged and bleak.

The Pennines are a chain of hills that run like a spine from northern England to the Midlands. Central and eastern England have mostly low plains. The Welsh landscape includes mountains in both the north and south.

The average annual temperature in Great Britain ranges from about 7°C in the far north to about 11°C on the Cornish coast in the south-west.

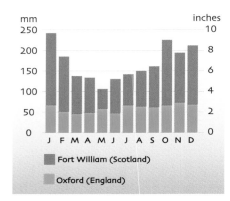

Above. **Rainfall each month in a town in Scotland and a town in England.**

Fort William (Scotland)

Oxford (England)

Summer Temperatures

December, January and February are the coldest months in Britain; June, July and August are the hottest months.

Surface temperature
in July

Over 60ºF	Over 16ºC
58-60º	15-16º
55-58º	13-15º
32-55º	0-13º

London

Animal Life

Great Britain's mammals include deer, squirrels, moles, badgers, foxes, rabbits, hares, mice, voles and bats. Among reptiles and amphibians are lizards, frogs, newts and toads. Birdlife includes several types of gulls, ducks, geese, tits and swans as well as ptarmigan, golden eagles and grey herons.

Web Search ▶▶

▶ www.met-office.gov.uk
Weather information from the Meteorological Office.

The People

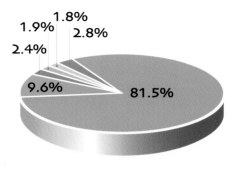

1.9% 1.8%
2.8%
2.4%
9.6%   81.5%

English   Scottish   Irish   Welsh
Ulster   West Indian, Indian, Pakistani and Oth

Above. **The original nationalities of the people of Great Britain.**

As well as the native Scots, Welsh and English, many other people have settled in Britain over the centuries.

Ancestors and language

The Scots and Welsh are descendants of the Celts, who settled the islands in prehistoric times. They now make up 12 per cent of the population. The English are a mix of the German, Danish and French people that arrived between about CE 400 and 1200.

After World War II, people from former British colonies such as India, Hong Kong and the West Indies were encouraged to come to Britain. They now make up 4.5 per cent of the population.

The country's official language is English. Around a quarter of people in Wales speak Welsh. Scots Gaelic is spoken by about 60,000 people.

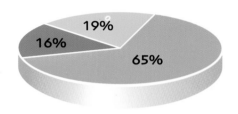

19%
16%
65%

0-14 Total 11.2million (Men 5.8m/Women 5.5m)
15-64 Total 38.5million (Men 19.4m/Women19.1
65 + Total 9.2million (Men 3.8m/Women 5.4m)

Above. **Numbers of men and women. Men live to about 75 years of age and women to about 80.**

Right. **At Speakers' Corner in London, people of any nationality, culture or religion can speak openly.**

Below. Immigrants granted British citizenship in 2000.

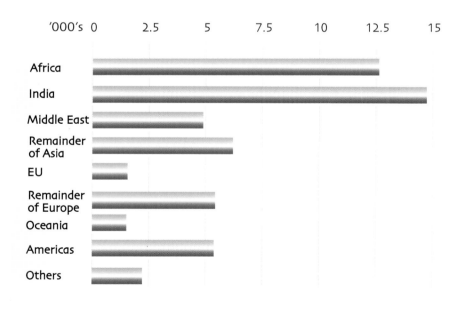

| '000's | 0 | 2.5 | 5 | 7.5 | 10 | 12.5 | 15 |

Africa
India
Middle East
Remainder of Asia
EU
Remainder of Europe
Oceania
Americas
Others

Above. Most British people live in the south-east of England. They travel to work by train, bus and car.

🌐 **Web Search** ▶▶

▶ www.statistics.gov.uk
Up-to-the-minute facts and figures about Great Britain and the United Kingdom.

▶ www.direct.gov.uk/Home page/fs/en
▶ www.wales.gov.uk
▶ www.scotland.gov.uk/
▶ www.discovernorthern ireland.com
Information on all parts of Britain and the United Kingdom.

Above. In the countryside, there are small cottages like these, as well as large country houses like the one shown on page 6.

Population Density

Great Britain has one of the world's highest numbers of people per square kilometre.

Population - people per sq. mile/km

2,600 or over	1000 or over
1500-2600	600-999
780-1500	300-599
390-780	150-299
under 390	under 150

Edinburgh

Manchester

Birmingham

Cardiff

London

Right. Traffic in London. London is the largest city in Great Britain with more than 7 million people.

Town and Country Life

Over 90 per cent of British people live in towns and cities. The country is twice as crowded as its neighbour, France.

Houses, shops and offices

Many people have moved to the countryside and travel into cities to work. As a result, new houses and shopping areas have grown around villages. In industrial cities built in the late 1800s you can still see rows of red-brick houses.

During the 1950s and 1960s, blocks of council-owned flats were built to fill areas destroyed by bombing in World War II. More recently, private homes have been built in the suburbs and in growing towns such as East Kilbride and Milton Keynes.

In the last 10 years, new houses, offices and shopping malls have been built in the run-down docklands of major cities, including London, Liverpool and Edinburgh.

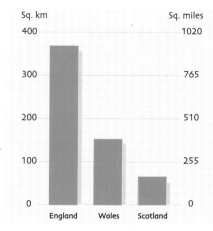

Above. **Population density (people per square kilometre).**

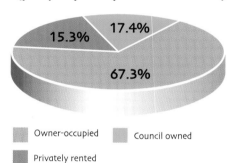

17.4%
15.3%
67.3%

Owner-occupied   Council owned

Privately rented

Above. **People who own or rent their houses.**

Web Search ►►

► www.streetmap.co.uk
Find and print a street map of any British town or village.

► www.dsdni.gov.uk/housing/introduction.asp
Facts and figures about houses and homes in Britain.

Farming and Fishing

Below. **A small fishing boat in a harbour.**

Low-lying land is mostly used to grow crops. Hills are used for grazing animals.

Crops and livestock

Britain's main crops are cereals (wheat, barley and oats), oilseed rape, sugar beet and potatoes. Fruit and vegetables are grown in south-east England.

Sheep and cattle are the most important livestock, followed by pigs and poultry. Wales is famous for its lamb and Scotland for its beef. Dairy products include milk, butter and cheese.

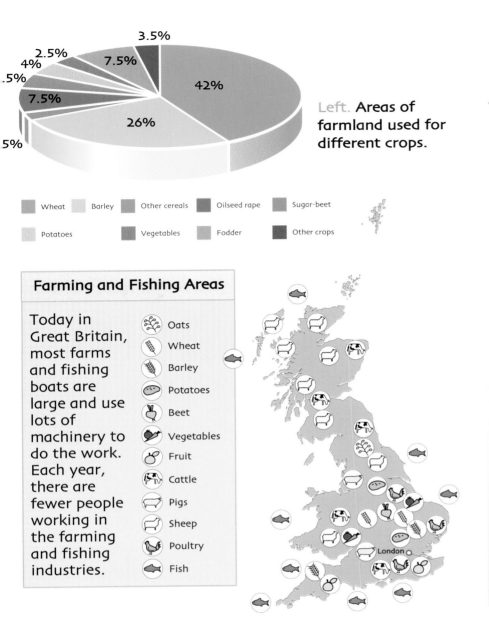

3.5%
2.5%
4%
.5%
7.5%
7.5%
5%
42%
26%
5%

Left. **Areas of farmland used for different crops.**

| | Wheat | | Barley | | Other cereals | | Oilseed rape | | Sugar-beet |
| | Potatoes | | Vegetables | | Fodder | | Other crops |

Farming and Fishing Areas

Today in Great Britain, most farms and fishing boats are large and use lots of machinery to do the work. Each year, there are fewer people working in the farming and fishing industries.

Oats
Wheat
Barley
Potatoes
Beet
Vegetables
Fruit
Cattle
Pigs
Sheep
Poultry
Fish

London

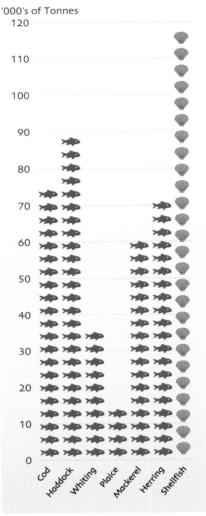

'000's of Tonnes

120
110
100
90
80
70
60
50
40
30
20
10
0

Cod Haddock Whiting Plaice Mackerel Herring Shellfish

Above. **Fish catches per year made by Great Britain's sea-going fishing boats.**

The fishing industry

There are more than 8,000 fishing boats in Britain. They catch over 600,000 tonnes of seafish a year, more than 65 per cent of the country's needs. Overfishing has reduced the numbers of fish caught, but the Dogger Bank in the North Sea remains one of the world's richest fishing grounds.

Web Search ▶▶

▶ www.defra.gov.uk/
Information about farming and fishing from the Department for Environment Food and Rural Affairs.

Resources and Industry

Great Britain is one of the world's top industrial countries. About 20 per cent of people work in manufacturing. This creates a quarter of the country's wealth.

Fuels, minerals and products

Britain produces 100 million tonnes of coal each year. Most of this coal is burned in power stations. With oil and gas in the North Sea, Britain has more energy resources than any other EU country. Its mineral resources include tin and zinc.

The main products of Britain's factories are electronics, cars, aircraft, chemicals, man-made fibres, foods and plastics.

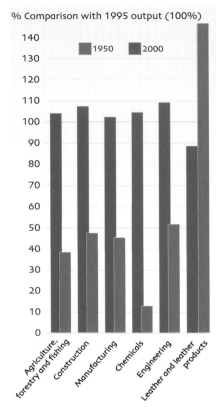

% Comparison with 1995 output (100%)

■ 1950　■ 2000

Agriculture, forestry and fishing; Construction; Manufacturing; Chemicals; Engineering; Leather and leather products

Above. **Rise and fall of the output of selected industries.**

All kinds of services

65 per cent of all workers work in service industries. They have jobs selling goods or giving help, advice and support. Examples of service industries are tourism, banking, computing and insurance. The number of shops, restaurants, fitness centres and banks grows each year.

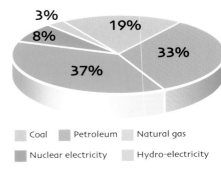

3%
19%
8%
33%
37%

Coal   Petroleum   Natural gas
Nuclear electricity   Hydro-electricity

Above. **Different energies used in 2000.**

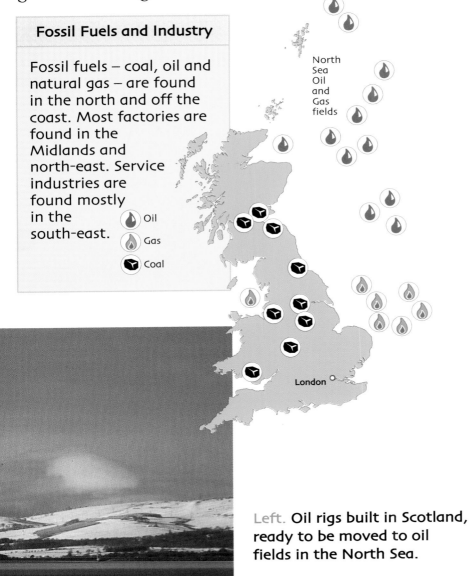

Fossil Fuels and Industry

Fossil fuels – coal, oil and natural gas – are found in the north and off the coast. Most factories are found in the Midlands and north-east. Service industries are found mostly in the south-east.

Oil
Gas
Coal

North Sea Oil and Gas fields

London

Left. **Oil rigs built in Scotland, ready to be moved to oil fields in the North Sea.**

Major changes

Since 1975, Britain's output of crude oil has increased 80 times, output of natural gas and nuclear electricity have trebled, while coal production has more than halved.

Today, Britain uses only 10 per cent more energy than it did in 1975. However, the industrial output has doubled. This is because its use of energy is far more efficient. Also, Britain's power stations produce far less pollution than they did in 1975.

Web Search ▶▶

▶ www.dti.gov.uk
The UK Department of Trade and Industry's website.

Transport

Britain's main transport routes are roads and motorways. There is also a big rail network, and airlines fly to most parts of the country.

Road and rail

In the 1900s, most goods were transported by trains and canal barges. Now, 65 per cent of goods are carried by lorries. The biggest road-users are car drivers. Some people travel to work by train. Others use buses, motorcycles and bicycles.

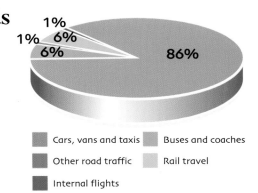

1%
1% 6%
6% 86%

- Cars, vans and taxis
- Buses and coaches
- Other road traffic
- Rail travel
- Internal flights

Above. **Travellers using each type of transport.**

Below. **Britain has 27.5 million registered road vehicles. Traffic jams are a common problem.**

Motorway Links

The major motorways run north-south, to Wales, and between Liverpool, Manchester and Leeds. The M25 opened in 1986. It is a circular motorway that allows heavy traffic to bypass the busy centre of London.

Edinburgh

Manchester

Birmingham

Cardiff

London

M25

Motorwaysh

Air and sea routes

Air traffic in Britain has increased a lot in recent years, and there are international airports in many British cities.

Cargo leaves and enters Britain mainly by ship. Ferries from Dover carry passengers to mainland Europe. Increasingly, though, cargo and passengers travel to mainland Europe by train through the Channel Tunnel which links Britain and France.

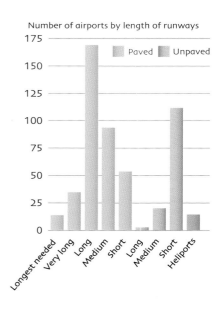

Above. **Britain's airports and heliports. Heathrow is Europe's busiest airport.**

Left. **Average distances people travel in a year by the main types of transport.**

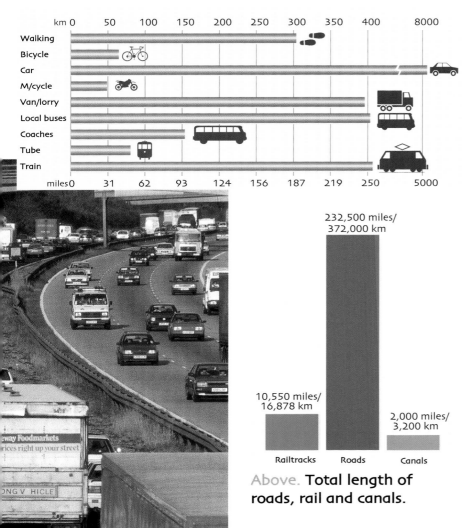

232,500 miles/ 372,000 km

10,550 miles/ 16,878 km

2,000 miles/ 3,200 km

Railtracks   Roads   Canals

Above. **Total length of roads, rail and canals.**

Web Search ▶▶

▶ **www.rail.co.uk**
Railway companies, their timetables and travel services.

▶ **www.theaa.co.uk**
The Automobile Association.

▶ **www.caa.co.uk**
The Civil Aviation Authority.

▶ **www.abports.co.uk**
The Association of British Ports.

Above. In many secondary schools, children must wear a uniform.

Left. Cambridge University is one of the oldest universities in Britain. It dates from the 13th century.

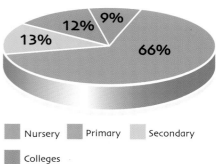

9%
12%
13%
66%

- Nursery
- Primary
- Secondary
- Colleges

Above. Number of schools at all levels.

Education

British children must go to school between the ages of 5 and 16. Education is free but some children go to private, fee-paying schools.

From nursery to university

Many children go to nursery school from the age of three. When they are five, children start primary school. Here they are taught mostly reading, writing and maths skills. There is a national curriculum for England and Wales. This means that schools teach the same subjects to the same levels of difficulty. Scotland has its own, similar system.

Most children over the age of 11 study a range of subjects at secondary school. Then, at age 14 or 15, they start to study for exams called GCSEs, or SSGs in Scotland. Children may then leave school or go to college to study further.

Students gain a university place based on their exam results. Many students take out loans to pay for their studies. Sometimes they receive money from the government.

DATABASE

TV Education
The Open University was set up in 1971. Its students do not go to classes, so they can study and have a job at the same time. Television and radio programmes back up the course work.

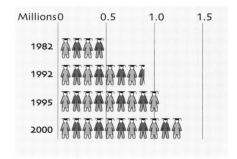

Above. **Growth in the number of students who go to university.**

Web Search ▶▶

▶ www.dfes.gov.uk
Information from Britain's Department for Education and Skills.

Sport and Leisure

Many of the world's most popular sports began in Britain, including football, rugby, golf, tennis and cricket.

Teams, clubs and competitions

To many, football is Britain's national sport. Teams such as Manchester United, Arsenal and Liverpool are world-famous.

Rugby originated at Rugby School in Warwickshire. Today, there are two versions of the game: rugby league and rugby union. Rugby league is played mainly in northern England. England, Scotland and Wales play rugby union at an international level. In 2003, England won the rugby union World Cup.

Scotland is the home of golf and England the home of tennis and cricket. The most important golf club is St Andrews near Dundee. The world's most famous tennis club, at Wimbledon, hosts a major tennis tournament each summer. Cricket is played throughout England. Internationals, called test matches, are played in the summer. Cricket is also played in the south of Wales.

Top Sports

Sports most commonly played at British schools are, in order:
1. Athletics –35 per cent of children
2. Gymnastics –33 per cent
3. Rounders (similar to baseball) –31 per cent
4. Swimming –30 per cent
5. Football –28 per cent

Above. **Bowls is a traditional British sport. It is played both indoors and outdoors.**

Above. Football internationals are played at larger stadiums across the country, including the Millennium Stadium in Cardiff, Wales, shown here.

Members '000's

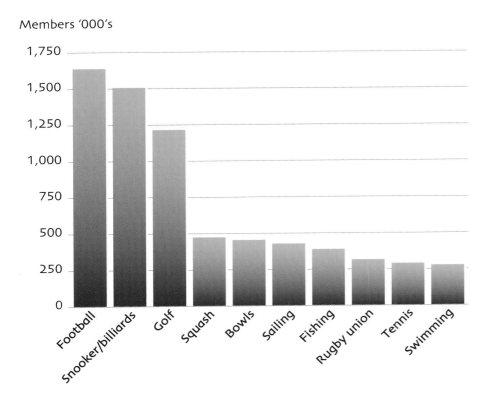

Left. The number of people belonging to sports clubs.

Web Search ▶▶

▶ www.culture.gov.uk
Government department for Culture, Media and Sport.

▶ www.sportengland.org
▶ www.ssc.org.uk
▶ www.sports-council-wales.
co.uk
England's, Scotland's, and Wales' sporting bodies.

Daily Life and Religion

In Britain, people usually go to school from Monday to Friday and work from 9 a.m. to 5.30 p.m. each day.

Relaxing and shopping

Watching TV and listening to the radio are the main forms of relaxation. Shopping is a popular weekend activity. People shop at local markets or in large shopping centres.

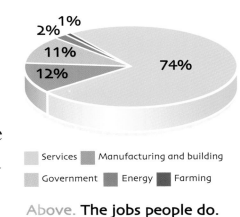

1%
2%
11%
12%
74%

Services — Manufacturing and building
Government — Energy — Farming

Above. **The jobs people do.**

Below. **A typical street market.**

Religion and healthcare

Most people in Britain are Christians. The Anglican Church is the state religion. Other Christian groups include Roman Catholics, Methodists, Presbyterians and Baptists. Britain has the second-largest Jewish community in Europe and growing communities of Muslims, Hindus and Sikhs.

Public healthcare is provided by the National Health Service (NHS). People can visit doctors, dentists and opticians and also receive free hospital treatment. There are also private hospitals and doctors paid for by medical insurance.

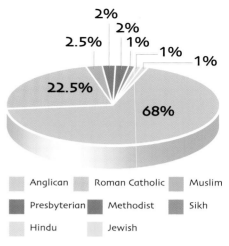

Anglican	Roman Catholic	Muslim
Presbyterian	Methodist	Sikh
Hindu	Jewish	

Above. **Percentages of people belonging to religions.**

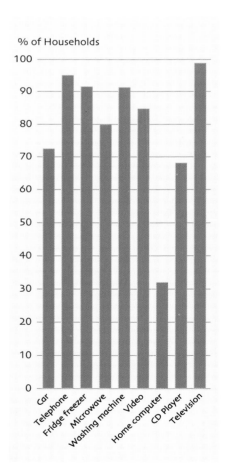

% of Households

Above. **Electrical goods owned by people in Britain.**

Above. **Towns such as Winchester in England are built around an historic cathedral.**

Arts and Media

Britain produces newspapers, books, plays, films and television programmes. It also has world-famous galleries and museums and specialist art collections.

Theatre, music and dance

London's West End is called 'theatreland'. The Cardiff and Edinburgh Festivals are two major events that take place each year. They are celebrations of dance, music and literature.

Below. **A street performance at the Edinburgh Festival.**

Web Search ▶▶

▶ www.britishtourist
   authority.org
   Links to all Britain's tourist attractions.

▶ www.scotlandonline.com/
   entertainment
   Exhibitions, concerts and movie reviews for Scotland.

▶ www.resource.gov.uk
   Britain's museum website.

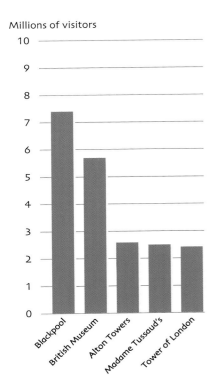

Millions of copies

4.0
3.5
3.0
2.5
2.0
1.5
1.0
0.5
0

The Sun | The Mirror | Daily Mail | Daily Express | Daily Telegraph | The Times | Daily Star | Guardian | Financial Times | Independent

Above. **More people in Britain read newpapers than anywhere else in the world.**

Millions of visitors

10
9
8
7
6
5
4
3
2
1
0

Blackpool | British Museum | Alton Towers | Madame Tussaud's | Tower of London

Film, literature, newspapers

The film industry in Britain is booming. Many films have been based on the works of British writers such as William Shakespeare and Charles Dickens.

The British Broadcasting Corporation (BBC) broadcasts two main television channels and five national radio stations. Channel 4, Channel 5 and ITV are independent television channels. Viewers can also watch satellite and cable television programmes from around the world. There are also many radio stations.

The most famous British newspapers are *The Times, The Mirror, The Sun* and *The Guardian.* The biggest-selling regional paper is the *Glasgow Daily Record.*

Left. **Millions of people visit Britain's tourist attractions.**

DATABASE

Famous Arts Institutions
- Birmingham Philharmonic Orchestra
- English National Opera
- Royal Ballet Company
- Royal Shakespeare Company
- Scottish Opera
- National Eisteddfod Society

Museums and Galleries
- Ashmolean Museum, Oxford
- British Museum, London
- Museum of Scotland, Edinburgh
- National Museum of Wales, Cardiff
- Tate Modern, London
- Tate, Liverpool
- Victoria and Albert Museum, London

Government

The queen is officially the head of state but Great Britain is actually governed by parliament. Members of Parliament (MPs) are elected by the British people.

Elections and parliaments

Elections are held once every five years, or sometimes more often. Everyone aged 18 or over may vote in elections.

Elected MPs sit in the House of Commons in London. Most MPs belong to the Conservative, Labour or Liberal Democratic Parties. The party that has the most MPs after an election forms a government. This is led by the Cabinet — a team of between 10 and 30 MPs and the prime minister, the leader of the ruling party.

British people also elect members to the European Parliament based in Brussels.

Below. The clock tower of the Houses of Parliament. There is also a Scottish Parliament and Welsh and Northern Ireland Assemblies. They deal with regional issues.

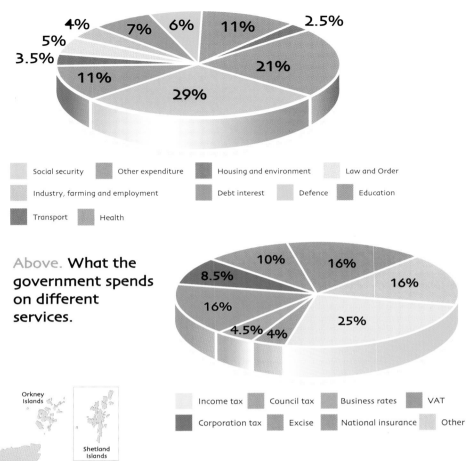

Social security	Other expenditure	Housing and environment	Law and Order
Industry, farming and employment	Debt interest	Defence	Education
Transport	Health		

Above. **What the government spends on different services.**

Income tax	Council tax	Business rates	VAT
Corporation tax	Excise	National insurance	Other

Above. **Government income from taxes.**

In Parliament

Decisions are made by a majority vote in parliament. There are two divisions, or 'houses', in parliament. Proposals, or Bills, are put to the House of Commons for MPs to vote on. Bills then go before the House of Lords. The Lords often suggest changes and these are usually added in. When a Bill has been voted for and agreed, it becomes an Act of Parliament and a law.

Local Government

Britain is divided into counties. The counties are each split into several boroughs. Each borough has its own council of locally elected members.

Major Counties

Other Authorities

Web Search ▶▶

▶ www.explore.parliament.uk
Introduction to the British parliament.

▶ www.royal.gov.uk
The official website of the British monarchy.

▶ www.scottish.parliament.uk/home.htm
Website of Scotland's Parliament.

▶ www.number-10.gov.uk
Features the history of the prime minister's home at No.10 Downing Street.

Important dates

CE 43 The Romans invade Britain

500s Angles, Saxons and Jutes settle

789 Viking raids

1066 Norman Conquest

1536 England and Wales formally united

1601 James VI of Scotland inherits English throne from Elizabeth I and becomes King James I

1640s English Civil War

1707 Act of Union between Scotland and England

1776 United States gains independence from Britain

1780s–1800s Industrial Revolution

1801 Ireland made part of the United Kingdom

1922 Republic of Ireland gains independence

1999 Welsh National Assembly and Scottish Parliament formed

Place in the World

In 1900, Great Britain had a huge empire. It had colonies all over the world. By 1970, most of its territories abroad were independent. Today, Great Britain is still a world power.

War and peace

In 1931, the British Empire became the Commonwealth. After World War II, it helped set up the United Nations. The UN's purpose is to maintain world peace.

Below. **Members of the British Royal Family in 2000, including Queen Elizabeth II and the Queen Mother (centre) and Prince Charles (second from right).**

28

Below. **Oxfam, a British aid relief charity, works with NATO forces in Kosovo.**

NATO and the EU

In 1949, Great Britain also founded the North Atlantic Treaty Organization (NATO), a military agreement with the United States and several European countries. In 1973, it joined the European Economic Community, which has since become the European Union (EU). This allows tourists, students and workers to travel and work between EU countries.

Although half of Britain's trade is with other EU countries, the United States is its single biggest trading partner. Many British people think of themselves as separate and different from continental Europeans.

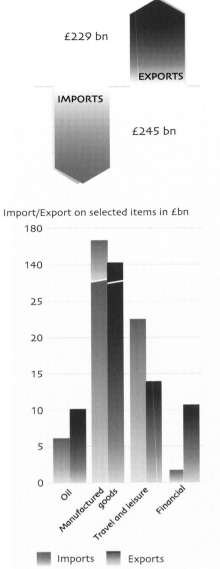

£229 bn

EXPORTS

IMPORTS

£245 bn

Import/Export on selected items in £bn

Imports   Exports

Above. **Major imports and exports.**

Web Search ▶▶

▶ www.nationalarchives.gov.uk/
The National Archives, which holds government and public documents.

Area:
229,991 sq km

Population size:
57,133,900

Capital city:
London (population 7,074,300)

Longest river:
Severn (354 km)

Highest mountain:
Ben Nevis (1,343 m)

Largest lake:
Loch Lomond (71 sq km)

Flag:
The UK's national flag is the Union Jack, which combines the crosses of St George of England (red cross on white background), St Andrew of Scotland (diagonal white cross on blue) and St Patrick of Ireland (diagonal red cross on white). The Welsh flag features a red dragon on a green and white background.

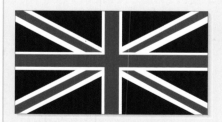

▲ Stonehenge, a prehistoric circle of stones in England.

Official language:
English

Currency:
Pound sterling (£)

Major resources:
Oil, gas, coal, tin, limestone, iron ore, salt, clay, chalk, gypsum, lead, silica

Major exports:
Manufactured goods, machinery, fuels, chemicals, transport equipment, financial services

National holidays and special events:
New Year's Day (1 January)
St David's Day (1 March)
Oxford v. Cambridge University Boat Race (last week in March)
Good Friday, Easter Sunday and Easter Monday (March or April)
St George's Day (23 April)
Early May Bank Holiday (first Monday in May)
Spring Bank Holiday (last Monday in May)
Queen's official birthday (June)
Edinburgh Festival (August)
Summer Bank Holiday (August)
Guy Fawkes' Day (5 November)
Remembrance Day (Sunday nearest 11 November)
St Andrew's Day (30 November)
Christmas Day (25 December)
Boxing Day (26 December)
New Year's Eve/Hogmanay (31 December)

Religions:
Anglican, Roman Catholic, Muslim, Presbyterian, Methodist, Sikh, Hindu, Jewish

Key Words

CLIMATE
The range of weather in a region over time.

COLONY
An area of land that is taken over, settled and ruled by another country.

COMMONWEALTH
A group of independent countries which were once part of the British Empire.

DOCKLANDS
An area in a city along a major river that was once the main port used by ships.

EMPIRE
A group of colonies ruled by a single country.

EXPORTS
Goods sold to a foreign country.

FERTILE
Land suitable for growing crops.

GOVERNMENT
The group of people who manage the country, deciding on its laws, raising taxes and organizing health, industry, farming, education, transport and other national systems and services.

GRAZING
Feeding on grass and shrubs in fields and open areas.

HYDRO-ELECTRIC ITY
Electrical power created from flowing water

IMMIGRANTS
People who come from one country to live in another.

IMPORTS
Goods bought from a foreign country.

KINGDOM
A territory ruled by a king or queen.

LIVESTOCK
Animals that are raised on a farm for their meat, milk, wool and skins.

MANUFACTURING
Using machinery to make products from raw materials.

NATIONAL CURRICULUM
The government plan for teaching, learning and testing subjects in schools.

NUCLEAR ELECTRICITY
Electricity produced by splitting atoms of uranium to release heat energy

PARLIAMENT
A seat of government. The UK parliament is divided into the House of Commons and the House of Lords.

POLLUTION
Damage to the environment.

POPULATION DENSITY
The average number of people living on a particular area of land.

PRINCIPALITY
A territory controlled by a prince (in the same way that a kingdom is controlled by a king or queen).

PROVINCE
A part of a country or state that has a certain identity.

RESOURCES
A country's supplies of energy, natural materials and minerals.

31

Index